WHERE WE LIVE

WE LIVE ON A PLANET

by Jennifer Boothroyd

Consultant: Beth Gambro
Reading Specialist, Yorkville, Illinois

Minneapolis, Minnesota

Teaching Tips

Before Reading

- Look at the cover of the book. Discuss the picture and the title.
- Ask readers to brainstorm a list of what they already know about the planet. What can they expect to see in the book?
- Go on a picture walk, looking through the pictures to discuss vocabulary and make predictions about the text.

During Reading

- Read for purpose. Encourage readers to think about planets as they are reading.
- Ask readers to look for the details of the book. What are they learning about life on Earth?
- If readers encounter an unknown word, ask them to look at the sounds in the word. Then, ask them to look at the rest of the page. Are there any clues to help them understand?

After Reading

- Encourage readers to pick a buddy and reread the book together.
- Ask readers to name two things they might see on our planet. Find the pages that tell about these things.
- Ask readers to write or draw something they learned about living on a planet.

Credits:
Cover and title page, © janrysavy/iStock, © kevron2001/iStock; 3, © janrysavy/iStock; 5, © dima_zel/iStock; 7, © titoOnz/Shutterstock; 8–9, © FrankRamspott/iStock; 10–11, © JGA/Shutterstock; 13, © Drazen_/iStock; 14–15, © hedgehog94/Adobe Stock; 16, © Wichyanan Limparungpatthanakij/iStock; 17, © FatCamera/iStock; 18–19, © Rawpixel.com/Adobe Stock; 20–21, © Wavebreakmedia/iStock; 22T, © robert_s/Shutterstock; 22M, © metha1819/Shutterstock; 22B, © Monkey Business/Adobe Stock; 23TL, © Fourleaflover/iStock; 23TR, © Tong Gao/iStock; 23BL, © Daisy-Daisy/iStock; 23BR, © kate_sept2004/iStock.

Library of Congress Cataloging-in-Publication Data is available at www.loc.gov or upon request from the publisher.

ISBN: 979-8-88822-063-4 (hardcover)
ISBN: 979-8-88822-260-7 (paperback)
ISBN: 979-8-88822-378-9 (ebook)

Copyright © 2024 Bearport Publishing Company. All rights reserved. No part of this publication may be reproduced in whole or in part, stored in any retrieval system, or transmitted in any form or by any means, electronic, mechanical, photocopying, recording, or otherwise, without written permission from the publisher.

For more information, write to Bearport Publishing, 5357 Penn Avenue South, Minneapolis, MN 55419.

Contents

Far from Earth 4

Planet Facts 22

Glossary 23

Index 24

Read More 24

Learn More Online 24

About the Author 24

Far from Earth

5, 4, 3, 2, 1!

The rocket lifts off.

It flies into the sky.

Soon, the ship is far above our planet.

Planets are big, round things in space.

They move around stars.

Earth is our planet.

It goes around a star we call the sun.

We have large areas of land on Earth.

They are called **continents**.

The waters around them are **oceans**.

Our planet is home to all kinds of living things.

Many plants and animals live on Earth.

There are billions of people here.

Luckily, this planet has everything we need to live.

It gives us air to breathe.

There is water to drink.

Earth takes care of us.

So, we need to take care of it back.

We can keep the planet clean.

What can we do to help?

Plant a tree.

Trees clean the air.

Animals can live in them.

Recycling makes less trash on Earth.

It turns something old into something new.

Reusing things is even better!

Try a water bottle you can use over and over.

We all share Earth.

And we can work together to take care of our planet.

It is where we live!

Planet Facts

There are 7 other planets that move around our sun. Earth is the only one with living things.

Dinos lived on Earth for 165 million years. People have lived here for less than 6 million.

Earth Day is a day all about our planet. People do things to take care of the planet.

Glossary

continents Earth's seven large land masses

oceans large bodies of salt water that cover Earth

recycling turning old things into new things

reusing doing something with an object again and again

Index

air 12, 16
animals 10, 16
continents 8–9
land 8
oceans 8
plants 10
water 8, 12, 18

Read More

Leed, Percy. *Earth: A First Look (Read for a Better World).* Minneapolis: Lerner Publications, 2023.

Rose, Rachel. *Planets (Off to Space!).* Minneapolis: Bearport Publishing Company, 2021.

Learn More Online

1. Go to **www.factsurfer.com** or scan the QR code below.
2. Enter **"On a Planet"** into the search box.
3. Click on the cover of this book to see a list of websites.

About the Author

Jenny Boothroyd loves seeing pictures of Earth from space. But she prefers to stay on Earth.